Christmas Gifts from the Heart

Dolley Carlson

illustrated by Kathleen O'malley

CVP

Chariot Victor Publishing
A Division of Cook Communications

Little book
be on your way

Bless the reader's
heart I pray

Chariot Victor Publishing
Cook Communications, Colorado Springs, CO 80918
Cook Communications, Paris, Ontario
Kingsway Communications, Eastbourne, England

CHRISTMAS GIFTS FROM THE HEART
© 1999 by Dolley Carlson for text.

3 1969 01154 9549

Designed by Brenda Franklin
Illustrated by Kathleen O'Malley
Edited by Julie Smith

First printing, 1999
Printed in Singapore
1 2 3 4 5 6 7 8 9 10 Printing/Year 03 02 01 00 99

Published in association with Yates & Yates, LLP, Literary Services, Orange, California.

. Library of Congress Cataloging-in-Publication Data

Carlson, Dolley
        Christmas gifts from the heart / by Dolley Carlson.
                p.   cm.
        ISBN 0-7814-3319-3
        1. Christmas. I. Title.
    GT4985.C28   1999
    394.2663--dc
                                        99-29792
                                        CIP

Unless otherwise noted, Scripture taken from the Holy Bible: New International Version©. Copyright © 1973, 1978, 1984 by International Bible Society. Used by permission of Zondervan Publishing House. All rights reserved. Other Scripture quotations taken from the Holy Bible, New Living Translation, (NLB) copyright © 1996. Used by permission of Tyndale House Publishers, Inc, Wheaton, Illinois 60189. All rights reserved; the King James Version (KJV).

Acknowledgments: An Irish Country Christmas, Alice Taylor, 1995, St. Martin's Press, NY; Come and Behold Him, Jack Hayford, 1995, Multnoman Books, Sisters, OR.

To my family and friends,
who make every day Christmas
with their gifts of love and joy!

God bless you, every one!

Thanks be to God
for his indescribable gift!

—2 Corinthians 9:15

Contents

Introduction

December is here! The blessed Christmas season . . . a time of great rejoicing and celebration! Remember what Christmas was like when you were a little child and could hardly wait to wake up on Christmas morning? You knew gifts were waiting for you . . . gifts carefully selected with lots of love. Christmas is a gift from the heart of God, heaven sent and lovingly given to the heart of all people.

*Christmas is when God came down
the stairs of heaven with a baby in His arms.
—Sterner*

My prayer is that through the pages of this little book you will discover—or rediscover—the childlike wonder, enthusiasm, and joy of Christmas.

*Backward, turn backward, O Time, in your flight,
make me a child again just for tonight!
— Elizabeth Akers Allen*

Come with me, let's walk through the days of Christmas together and prepare to embrace the love, peace, and joy that came long ago to Bethlehem. Let us be "wise" men and women carrying Christmas gifts from the heart to our family, friends, and community.

Let every heart prepare Him room

My Christmas Prayer for December 1st
Please, Lord, let my days be honoring to you . . .
prudent, serving, full of joy and love.
And, well, a little extra energy would be appreciated too!
Amen

Pray–Ponder–Plan

At Christmas play and make good cheer, for Christmas comes but once a year.
—Thomas Tusser

Between Thanksgiving and December first, Christmas still seems so far away. But it's not. . . . The weekend following Thanksgiving is perfect for praying, pondering, and planning for Christmas.

But Mary treasured up all these things and pondered them in her heart. —Luke 2:19

We can learn from Mary's wonderful example of pondering as we prepare for Christmas celebrations, traditions, and gifts.

Treasure Up and Ponder . . .

. . . how to make a warm, joyous, and meaningful Christmas for our family and friends.

. . . how much time, energy, and financial resources we have to make Christmas happen.

. . . the gifts of forgiveness, love, and hope that the Christ Child brought to us.

. . . and treasure the present moment. This Christmas will never happen again. This is it, our opportunity to give Christmas gifts of hospitality, care, generosity, and joy.

Bring your Christmas before the One whose birth we celebrate. Pray and ask Jesus what kind of celebration He wants in your home, listen for His answer, and begin to plan.

7

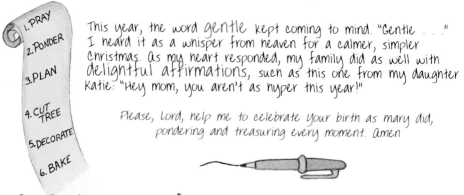

1. PRAY
2. PONDER
3. PLAN
4. CUT TREE
5. DECORATE
6. BAKE

This year, the word *gentle* kept coming to mind. "Gentle . . ." I heard it as a whisper from heaven for a calmer, simpler Christmas. As my heart responded, my family did as well with *delightful affirmations*, such as this one from my daughter Katie: "Hey mom, you aren't as hyper this year!"

Please, Lord, help me to celebrate Your birth as Mary did, pondering and treasuring every moment. Amen

The Practical Aspect of P.P.&P!

Every Christmas I buy a small red or green spiral notebook with pocket dividers (for coupons and ads). I write down everything I need to do for Christmas and everything that comes up along the way. And a large envelope holds every Christmas receipt. These really do help!

Remember, we need a little *grace and space* during the busy holiday season. The coziest space is home, and the grace comes with a good meal and no other commitments but to enjoy!

Bless this house O Lord we pray, keep it safe by night and day.

You can *bless* your home with prayer for Christmas and the whole year, too. Go outside and bless the path that leads up to your home, pray for the people who will walk on it. Bless the front door that all who enter may feel welcomed and loved, the kitchen and thank God for His provision, the family room and thank God for your family. Speak your *heart* to God in prayer for every room of your home and the garden too!

I do my best planning while sitting with a hot cup of tea. My favorite "*little something*" to go with it is Irish soda bread. My Uncle Johnny's is the best and here's the recipe just for you!

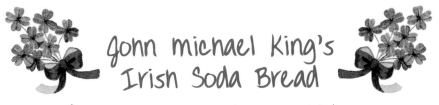

John Michael King's
Irish Soda Bread

2 1/2 cups flour
2 tsp. baking powder
1 tsp. salt
1/2 tsp. baking soda
1/4 cup butter (room temperature)

1/2 cup granulated sugar
1 egg slightly beaten
1 1/2 cups buttermilk (room temperature)
1 cup raisins
3 tbs. melted butter

Preheat oven to 375 degrees. Spray the inside of a 1 1/2-quart casserole with Pam.

Sift together the flour, baking powder, salt, and soda. Set aside. Cream butter and sugar, add beaten egg and buttermilk, blend. Add the liquid mixture to the dry ingredients and mix gently with an electric mixer on low speed or hand mix until well moistened. Fold in the raisins. Pour into casserole dish, drizzle melted butter evenly over the top, and sprinkle with sugar.

Bake at 375 degrees for 30 minutes; reduce to 325 degrees and bake for 30 more minutes. Check doneness by inserting a knife into the middle. If it comes out clean, your bread is done! Serve warm with lots of butter! It's also delicious "top o' the mornin'" on Christmas Day!

Irish Soda Bread as a Gift

The above recipe can be divided into two smaller casseroles (less baking time—watch closely). After cooling, wrap in cellophane, tie with a pretty ribbon, and attach a little note of blessing!

God bless hands that impart
Baked-good blessings
From the heart.

"FOR YOU WITH LOVE"

What to Give for Christmas?

One gift, two gifts, three gifts, four . . .
what to give for Christmas and a whole lot more.

GRACE

GENEROSITY

LOVE

JOY

HUMILITY

RESPECT

HOPE

PROMISE

Dear Jesus,
Thank You for the gift of Christmas! Please help me to do Christmas as You would, Lord, with Surprise Gifts of goodness, humility, and servant love when least expected. Needed Gifts of food, clothing, dignity, promise, and respect. Wanted Gifts of something so special, a tangible gift perhaps, something dreamt of but never expected. O Lord, lead me to give this way to the person who has lost hope, lost joy, lost promise. I so want to reflect the one who dwells within my heart. In Your care and waiting for directions,

Dolley

Gift Ideas

On the first day of Christmas, my true love gave to me . . .

One of the best pictures I have of my husband was taken the first Christmas we stayed within the budget. People comment, "He looks so happy." And every Christmas he says, "Can we take a picture like that of me this year, honey?"

This chapter and the next hold many gift ideas . . . gifts to be made, baked in your kitchen, and some "creative purchases." You'll also find ideas for intangible "love gifts" straight from your heart. Let's begin with . . .

A Vintage Family Picture

My friend Anne gave her brother a beautiful picture of their mother, who now makes her home in heaven. He was thrilled to receive this family treasure, and Anne wondered "what other things I have in my attic that could be a blessing to my brothers?" It's the kind of gift that only you can give, dear reader. It can't be purchased. How about some "home shopping" this year?

A Little Heart-shaped Potpourri Pillow

My mother-in-law gave me 2 of her mother's dining room chairs. I had them reupholstered, the old fabric dry-cleaned, and then made potpourri hearts (about 8", trimmed with crocheted cotton lace, and a ribbon loop for hanging) for the ladies in our family. When Grandma (my mother-in-law) opened her present she said, "Oh, I love potpourri." At second glance she exclaimed, "Oh, my mother's dining room fabric! Dolley, this is wonderful, thank you!" It made me happy to see her so happy.

Soup's On!

A friend put assorted beans and a small pack of seasoning in a large food-storage bag. Several strings of raffia held it all together, and the recipe was attached as well. I loved her creativity and practicality!

Bathrobes

One Christmas I made robes for our 3 nephews and hemmed them on the way to our Christmas Eve celebration. Whew! They were a big hit and the boys wore those robes for years. The robes were far from perfect, but from my heart, and the boys' gift was loving and wearing them anyway!

Wooden Christmas Decorations

Our collection of "Grandpa" designs includes a flying angel, a reindeer planter, and a wooden candle holder with red poinsettias. Grandma was the official painter for "Santa's Workshop" The first Christmas Grandpa made his home in heaven we missed him terribly. Grandma surprised us all with one more of their mutual Christmas decoration creations, a very pretty Swedish midsummer pole centerpiece.

Especially for Children

The unfinished furniture store is a treasure trove of gifts. Lorayne, a family friend, spent the summer painting gifts from the heart for her grandchildren. Here are some of her ideas.

Rocking Chairs

Paint the chairs white with the child's name in block letters. Then individualize each chair with its own design. The sky's the limit! Underneath each chair she wrote in black ink, "Handpainted for (child's name) by Grandma—Christmas 1998."

What a Doll

Lorayne bought doll houses that were similar to those her darling grandaughters live in. Each mom eagerly donated the same paint that was on their real homes for Grandma's wonderful creation.

"I Think I Can, I Think I Can"

Unfinished wooden train sets were purchased, and Lorayne went to work painting and creating heirloom gifts from the heart for her grandsons. Remember to sign and date everything you create!

Gifts for Our Dear Senior Citizens

Old age: the crown of life . . . —Cicero

Help—A Gift of Time

Shopping for presents · wrapping presents · mailing presents and Christmas cards · Telephone, cards, and letters · make calls to them, send cards, and write letters—lots!

"MY TIME IS YOUR TIME"

A Special Christmas Outing Such As

A concert · A night of seeing Christmas lights · A lunch or dinner out · A holiday parade · A Christmas tea · A visit to an old friend. Old friends are often isolated from each other because of transportation needs. · A holiday church service

And we regard thee dear ones as kings and queens of wisdom, love, and understanding. Thank you, thank you!

Presents

Stamps and stationery · Ice packs and shelf reachers (Grandma says so) · Gift certificates for restaurants, grocery stores, and pharmacies · Coupon good for one day's worth of errands · Purse or wallet · Book in large print · magnifying glass · Address book · Teddy bear!

Think whimsy, think comfort, think respect, think joy, think honor, think fun when you're considering a Christmas gift from the heart for the elderly person in your life.

COUPON

"LET'S HAVE TEA!"

Ideas . . . Ideas . . . Ideas . . .

A "Hectic Holiday Meal" (to go in the freezer or be eaten right away)

A Piece of Costume Jewelry (give her hearts, elephants, bicycles, apples . . .)

Frame a Letter, certificate, award, Diploma (two gifts in one, actually, framing and honor too!)

Store Certificates for Coffee, fast food, or Ice Cream. (Surprise a helpful clerk with a certificate for a treat!)

A Christmas Decoration (cookie cutters with recipe, salt and pepper set, Christmas plate . . .)

Gift Certificate to a Driving Range or a miniature Golf Course (you'll hit a hole in one!)

WATER COLOR PAPER

A Box of Watercolors and Paper (validates the talent you know is there!)

A Planned Day Trip (for the person who needs you to step in and help with a day off)

Buy or make Christmas Stockings for your children or Grandchildren

ideas ideas ideas ideas ideas ideas

. . . Ideas . . . and more Ideas!

a Bible Every good gift and every perfect gift is from above, coming down from the Father— James 1:17

Homemade Doll Clothes or Doll Furniture

afghans or Quilts (through the years Grandma has made one for every grandchild, six in all.)

Send Cookies to your Loved One Far away

a Gift Pack of fancy Jams or Candies or cheese and crackers (or whatever their fancy is!)

a Box of assorted Chocolates (no one ever said no to a box of chocolates)

museum or Home Tour and Dessert afterwards

Begin a Collection . . . . Christmas Dishes (one piece each year) . . . an Angel . . . a Child's Toy for an adult (I gave Candy a red-plaid lunch box this year. She takes it to her office every day!)

The Same Gift for Everyone It really simplifies things. To help you get started . . . a Christmas Teapot . . . a Pretty Vase . . . a Little Pitcher, Pancake mix, and maple Syrup for Christmas morning breakfast . . . a Christmas Throw Pillow . . . a Christmas Ornament . . . a Christmas Devotional . . . a Decorative Christmas Plate

Baked Gifts from your Kitchen

Delight yourself in the Lord and he will give you the desires of your heart.—Psalm 37:4

Perfect Sugar Cookies
Get out your cookie cutters, and plan an afternoon of making and baking your Christmas gift from the heart. Pack them in gift tins, gift bags, gift boxes, or simply on a pretty paper plate wrapped in cellophane and tied with a ribbon! You'll find the recipe in the "Memories and Traditions" chapter, cookie!

Christmas Breads
It's been years since I made Carrot Bread for gifts, but my friend Carol assures me that it "has to go in the book, it's absolutely delicious." She loves the aroma when it's baking. Must be the cinnamon, nutmeg, and cloves.

Irish Soda Bread—Uncle Johnny's Recipe
This makes a really good gift, especially to your friends with a wee bit o' Irish in them! You'll be findin' the recipe in the "Pray–Ponder–Plan" chapter.

God bless you and God bless me
and God bless soda bread and tea!

Strawberry Trifle
This delicious combination of butter cake, vanilla custard, strawberries, and whipped cream makes a lovely-to-look-at dessert gift. You're invited to the "Christmas Parties and Gatherings" chapter for the recipe!

16

Dolley's Carrot Bread

Preheat oven to 300 degrees Spray 2 loaf pans with Pam.
Combine the following three ingredients and bring to a boil:

1 1/2 cups water   1 cup grated carrots   2 tbs. shortening

Add these spices and boil for 10 minutes:

1 tsp. cinnamon   1 tsp. ground cloves   1 tsp. nutmeg

Add 1 cup raisins to above ingredients and boil for 5 more minutes.
Watch closely and gently stir from time to time.

Sift together these dry ingredients and set aside:

1 1/2 cups granulated sugar   2 tsp. baking soda
2 cups flour   1/2 tsp. salt

Beat 2 eggs and add to the dry ingredients. Mix together. Add 1 cup crushed
nuts—pecans or walnuts or almonds—to the dry ingredients. Gently and thoroughly mix everything together. Put mixture into 2 loaf pans and sprinkle with brown sugar.
Bake in a 300-degree oven for 1 hour. Cool slightly, remove from loaf pan, and cool
completely on a wire rack.

And sometimes we need to make what I call a "Creative Purchase"!

Bakery Boxes Hold Such Sweet Treasures . . . "What's inside,
what's inside?" my children would gleefully ask when I came home with
one. A bakery is a great place to pick up a Christmas gift from the
heart.

Pat-a-cake, pat-a- cake, baker's man,
bake me a cake as fast as you can . . .

17

Gifts That Money Can't Buy

*The joy of brightening other lives, bearing each others' burdens,
easing others' loads and supplanting empty hearts and lives
with generous gifts becomes for us the magic of Christmas.*
—W.C. Jones

Grandma always has a few special gifts for Christmas morning. One year my gift came in a candy box. But it wasn't filled with chocolates, it was filled with family treasures . . . two beautiful blue and white candles from Denmark purchased 10 years before, but "they're just too pretty to burn, and I wanted you to have them." And 10 tiny angels that were Christmas decorations in my husband's boyhood home. And 8 little golden bow ornaments that had belonged to Grandma's mother, Tillie Ohlund. My gift this year was a lovely little china vase, given to her and Grandpa on their 50th wedding anniversary. It means so much . . . And I love it!

These are gifts that can't be purchased, such treasures are priceless!
"Gifts that mean the most don't need to cost the most."

I Have No Money, What Can I Give?

A teacher told me about a Christmas gift she received from a refugee student whose family escaped a nation in great turmoil. "They are very poor." In a very sweet Christmas card, the student wrote of love and appreciation for her teacher who, at second glance, noticed names on the card other than her student's. She learned that the student had found used Christmas cards and "made them her own," finding a way to give appreciation and Christmas love. What someone else had discarded became her gift from the heart.

18

Gift Certificates from the Heart

The heart of the giver makes the gift dear and precious.—Martin Luther

Some of the most **memorable** gifts Tom and I have received were "love gift" redeemable coupons. When our daughters were quite young, we were in a Bible study, and drew names for Christmas "love gifts", that is, gifts of time and service.

Brian drew my name, and his gift was 4 coupons for baby-sitting. He made the coupons with construction paper, crayons, and stars. Such creativity! When Brian took care of the girls we knew they would be safe, really safe. He played football in college and was huge! The Lord sent us a wonderful caregiver and protector in our friend and baby-sitter Brian.

Coupons and Certificates

Make one or several and put them in an envelope. Be sure to decorate everything!

Supplies

Any paper, envelopes, frames, or tubes. Lots of crayons, paste, magazine pictures, photos, markers, glitter, stickers, stamps, ribbon, raffia, buttons, charms, candy. You can use just about anything! It's the **heart's intent** and love that matter most! Now take a little time, get a snack, put your feet up, and consider what might make a surprising and delightful "love gift."

Later on we'll conspire—As we dream by the fire—
To face unafraid, the plans that we made,
walkin' in a winter wonderland!

This coupon or certificate

Driving Carpool . . . Your turn becomes mine!

Washing the Dog . . . Glue a hotel sized soap here!

An Afternoon of Yard Work . . . Glue a seed packet to this one!

A Weekend of Baby-sitting—Or one Baby-sitting Job . . . Pin a diaper pin to this coupon!

An Afternoon of How-To . . . Computer Lessons

One Weekend Away at Home . . . This is great for a husband or wife to give to each other, especially if the budget is really tight and even if it isn't.

I'll arrange everything . . . The calendar, the baby-sitting (trade this with another couple), what we'll do, and the menu too!

Help with the Clutter—Basement, Closets, or Garage . . . You need a partner for this!

Mending . . . Glue a needle and thread on this coupon!

Three Hours of a Helping Hand . . . You Choose!

A Picnic . . . You Pick the Time and Place . . .

An Old-Fashioned Pot Roast Dinner for Eight . . . Invite the People, Pick the Date!

A Pasta Dinner for Six . . . You Pick the Time and Friends, I'll "maka" the Pasta! . . .

Vacuuming the Whole House . . . Emptying the Dishwasher . . . Filling the Dishwasher . . . Packing Lunches

is redeemable for . . .

Tea for Two—Just me and you! or . . . a Tea Party for Four—You pick the time and friends, I'll put the kettle on! . . . Paste or staple a teabag on these last two suggestions.

You can also make coupons and certificates for children. They make great stocking stuffers!

One friend to Spend the night . . .

Good for One Bed made . . . no chores Today!

An After School Pizza Party . . . for you and your friends

A Teddy Bear Tea Party . . .

A Tent Sleepover in the Backyard . . . 4 friends

Time for You and a friend . . . at the Batting cages

Ice-cream monday Party . . .

A trip to the skateboard Park . . . with 3 friends

Follow your heart for additional gift ideas and coupon creations! You'll have a lot of fun with this, and the possibilities for delight and surprise are endless. The Lord's loving presence in our hearts miraculously transforms us from mere mortals to vessels of His love. Blessings abound when the family of God is at work dispensing gifts from the heart.

God has given gifts to each of you from his great variety of spiritual gifts. manage them well so that God's generosity can flow through you.
— 1 Peter 4:10 NLB

more Gifts that money Can't Buy

The manner of giving is worth more than the gift.—Pierre Corneille

Grace

I broke my glasses and had to buy department store substitutes until I could see the eye doctor. On returning home, the glasses were missing. I called the store, and on about the 12th ring the clerk shouted into the phone, "This better be really important!" For some inexplicable reason, I let it go! And you know, dear reader, it felt right, really right. It was Christmas, and this lady had probably been on her feet for at least 8 hours. According to webster grace means "unmerited good will or clemency . . . the divine influence acting within the heart." That's it, that's what we're looking for!

On the weather outside is frightful and the fire is so delightful . . .
Let it snow, let it snow, let it snow!

On a confrontation is frightful and your gracious heart delightful . . .
let it go, let it go, let it go!

Let Your Words Be Gifts

affirm, befriend, encourage, sympathize, empathize, comfort. Say hello, say goodbye, say I'm sorry, say I'll get that for you, do you want something to eat? How about a cup of tea? you look so pretty/handsome, that was delicious, do you need some help? Say merry Christmas, Happy New Year, say I love you!

may the words of my mouth and the meditation of my heart
be pleasing in your sight, O Lord.—Psalm 19:14

Care for Those Who Are Hurting

Do you know a family who will be spending their first Christmas without a loved one? Our first Christmas without Grandpa was so unlike all the others. Everything was the same, but Grandpa wasn't there. And we missed him terribly. I lost my own parents at an early age, and still every time I hear "Silent Night" a rush of childhood Christmas memories fills my heart with joy and my eyes with tears.

Our friends Dick and Teri lost their youngest son David to leukemia when he was just 4. Teri shared what was of comfort those first couple of years:

As a family, they have to do Christmas. Help them with the tree, decorating, Christmas cards, and shopping.

David's soccer coach wanted to help and offered his family cabin to us for a Christmas getaway. The love in his heart met the sorrow in ours and provided a place of comfort and solace for Dick, Brian, and me.

Include them in social gatherings—reassure them that they won't ruin the party.

A journal . . . helps . . . a lot.

At the close of our conversation I reminisced with Teri about David. She laughed gently and added , "Also tell people to send or speak a memory they have about the deceased. Dolley, I still love to hear those things."

So I leave it with you, dear reader, to comfort those in need with a gift from the heart. God bless your way.

Dios te tenga en su santa mano.
God keep you in His holy hand.—Anonymous

Christmas Cards—who, How, & why?

Every year we send a Christmas card (well, almost every year—we'll talk about that later).

Christmas Cards—Sent To . . .

Your card and its message could be quite timely, you never know. A Christmas card is a gift, to the heart, and its very being says, "You mean something to me and mine and we wanted to send Christmas greetings to you and yours!"

Christmas Card—How?

Snap a Picture: Attach the photo inside with double-sided tape. Some cards are designed specifically to hold a photo, or you can have a photo-all-in-one card made wherever you have film developed.

Ideas for a Christmas Photo: Buying the Christmas tree · The day the new baby came home · A special party or vacation · The whole family · Just the children · Grandma and grandpa and grandchildren · The latest family reunion, graduation, or wedding . . .

One year, my cousin Robin sent a close up photo card of her son Zak. His smile had two front teeth missing, as in "all I want for Christmas . . ."!

Create a Card: You can do this with the help of your children. Have card stock cut into postcard or greeting card size (you can fold it), buy appropriate-sized envelopes. Have stamps, pens, pictures, rubber stamps and pads handy. A home computer offers endless design possibilities. Selection of paper, design, and message can be a lot of fun! You can even scan in a photo!

Ready-made Christmas Postcards:
Less time and postage. No envelopes to stuff or lick . . . just a greeting, signature, and address, completed!

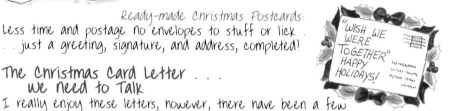

The Christmas Card Letter . . .
we need to Talk

I really enjoy these letters, however, there have been a few . . . Remember this is about greetings, news, and love. A couple of years ago my husband wrote our letter. It had 12 lines, 3 for each family member. Your Christmas letter doesn't need to be that brief. Have fun with it, but as you're writing please remember to check your heart motive. If it begins to sound like bragging there's a good chance it won't be read, and the opportunity for blessing and connecting will have been missed.

God bless us, everyone!—Tiny Tim

No Time for Christmas Cards This Year?

God rest ye merry, gentlemen (and women)
Let nothing you dismay . . .

Well, first of all, it's perfectly all right, some years are like that! Send a New Year, Valentine's or Easter card. It's keeping in touch that is most appreciated.

O Christmas Tree,
O Christmas Tree!

God made all kinds of trees grow out of the ground—
trees that were pleasing to the eye . . . —Genesis 2:9

This year we purchased 4 Christmas trees for our home.
Wildly extravagant? Please let me explain. At the cut-
your-own tree farm there were some very small
"Charlie Brown" trees. One was only $1 and another $4!
The third tree was adolescent size and the fourth—for
the living room—was the largest. They were graduated in
size and looked just like a little family. My
husband, Tom, said, "We can't break up the family!"

Their fresh pine fragrance permeates everything!
Katie looked at the unadorned trees, and said, "Mom,
let's keep it simple and just put lights and a star on
them this year." My friend Brenda says, "There's almost
something holy about a tree that simply decorated."
I believe there is too.

The Living Room Tree

It has only little white lights and an angel on top.
Traditionally we cover this tree in continuous trails
of gold and white ribbon wound round and up and
down (think roller coaster), gold and white ornaments,
and birds' nests sprinkled with a bit of gold
tinsel. The reward for all that decorating comes
with the placement of our tree-top angel. And
then . . . . the lights are plugged in and . . . another
Christmas has begun!

Dearest Jesus, "this little light of mine" may it shine
with the warmth of your love.

26

A Small Tree in the Family Room

This has always been our children's tree, and we loved the way they decorated with so much joy and whimsy. The last decorations . . . candy canes. So cute!

After the children were grown, we decorated the small tree with tiny white lights, stuffed animals, dolls, doll sleds and chairs—popping them in among the branches. Quick décor and fun too! A small, worn—but charming—quilt serves every year as the tree skirt.

A "Picture Perfect" Tree

For years, I've saved Christmas card photos. I just can't bring myself to throw them away, and now you don't have to either! Michelle came up with a unique idea for all those precious pictures. Trim each card picture into the shape of a Christmas ball. Laminate it (you can also use clear Contact paper). Punch a hole in the top and attach a small ornament hook or pull a ribbon, yarn, or twine through each one. Now you have picture-perfect ornaments!

The Littlest Tree

When our daughters were little girls we bought a small live pine tree and planted it in a wooden tub. Every Christmas it was carried into the house, decorated, then undecorated, and returned to the garden. One year it was too large to carry, so we planted it and now have a beautiful 20-foot pine tree. It's a sweet reminder of Christmas past.

Poems are made by fools like me,
but only God can make a tree.
—Joyce Kilmer

27

My First Christmas Tree—
What Will I Do For Ornaments?

*Maybe this is your very first Christmas
with your own tree to decorate and ornaments are few.
Here's a riddle just for you!*

Riddle: Your Christmas ornaments will come in the mail, each one shiny new and one-by-one as they arrive, intended just for you! Know the answer? Give up?

They're Christmas cards! As each one arrives, punch a hole in the upper left corner, pull a ribbon or yarn or twine (for a country look) through, tie the card in the tree, away from lights, and enjoy the vision of Christmas greetings from family and friends. Oh, and as an extra blessing all around, say a little prayer for the sender of each card!

*Let the trees of the forest rustle with praise.
—Psalm 96:12 NLT*

And This Is the Surprise Tree—Ready?
A small tree in the corner of your bedroom. It's so cozy and romantic, decorated only with tiny, white lights and a star on top. I used a heavy cotton lace valance (bunched and fluffed) for the tree skirt.

A Tree for the Infirm or Senior Citizen
Many of the catalogs that fill our mailboxes offer tabletop trees for Christmas. If you know someone who is in poor health or too elderly to decorate for Christmas, this is a delightful way to send Christmas love and care!

FROM:

TO:

Christmas Tree Skirts

Be very creative here. Look around your home. A tree skirt could be . . . a baby blanket, crocheted afghan, or quilt · a large piece of fabric—just bunch and fluff in place (I've done this with gold quilted fabric around the living room tree for years) · a favorite tablecloth or lace curtain or yards of white tulle look heavenly!

> Keep a green tree in your heart
> and perhaps the singing bird will come.—Chinese proverb

maybe a Tree Decorating Party?

Our friends Peter and Gail have one every year. Their "trim the tree" party truly is a Christmas gift from the heart with lots of good food, Christmas music, and best of all, love and friendship. They have almost the same guest list year in and year out and delight in watching children grow up right before their very eyes.

> Christmas gatherings from the heart
> To a child's memory will impart
> Love and music, food and joy
> Blessing every girl and boy!

Personally, I consider anyone who helps deck the halls an angel! And so I created the Candy Cane Angel Food Cake as a special dessert for my helpers. I hope your "angels" enjoy it as much as mine have!

29

Candy Cane Angel Food Cake

One box of angel food cake mix
1 pint heavy whipping cream
Powdered sugar to taste—this is the privilege of the
baker, tasting and testing, mmm!
Stabilizer for whipped cream—it will give the cream
a little more body and keep it firm for hours.
This product can usually be found in import specialty or
cake-decorating supply stores. (Don't worry,
you can make the cake without it.)
A package of candy canes.
A length of red ribbon—about 14 inches

Bake the cake according to directions and cool thoroughly.

Whip the cream until peaks begin to form and then slowly add powdered sugar. If you use the stabilizer follow the directions on the
package. Continue whipping the cream until stiff—but not too stiff.
We don't want butter! Now frost the angel food cake with the
whipped cream.

Press the candy canes into the side of the cake vertically, like little
marching soldiers. Don't put them too close together or you won't be
able to cut the cake. Or create your own pattern. Now crisscross two
more candy canes on the cake top. On the
opposite side of the cake top place a red
ribbon that you have already tied into a
bow. That's right, just put it on the
whipped cream and curly-cue the ribbon
around the top until about 2 inches from
the candy canes.

Angel food for your angel helpers,
guests, family, and friends!
Enjoy!

Decking the Halls

*Simply beautiful or beautifully simple!
We have the freedom to decorate a little or a lot.*

Festive decorations are a gift from your heart to the hearts of those who enter your home. They simply and sweetly say, "love lives here" and "we were expecting you, welcome!"

"Decking the halls" is one of the first traditions to take place at Christmastime. We collect ornaments and other decorations year by year and look forward to transforming our homes from the ordinary in celebration of the extraordinary, the birth of Jesus, Son of God, Christmas!

Some years we can do a lot of decorating and others, just a little. It's very easy to slip into the expectation of having our homes look like those we see in magazines. The reality is, we work part or full time, have a family to take care of, or aged parents to look after, and are involved in church and community activities. We need to bring expectation and reality as close together as possible in order to squeeze out depression. No holiday blues here, we're walking toward Christmas with realistic expectation, celebration, and enjoyment!

I will honor Christmas in my heart, and try to keep it all the year.
—Charles Dickens

Christmas—Beautifully Simple!

In the delightful little book *An Irish Country Christmas*, Alice Taylor draws heartfelt stories from her family and community experiences. I loved the sweet simplicity of their Irish decorations. They used holly, greens, a large white candle for one window at the front of the house, an especially grand log (yule log) for the back of the fireplace, Christmas cards, and most importantly a little creche (nativity scene) to honor the baby Jesus.

Away in a manger, no crib for His bed,
the little Lord Jesus laid down His sweet head.

Christmas—Simply Beautiful!

Pastor Jack Hayford encourages the reader of his Christmas devotional, *O Come Let Us Adore Him*, to do a lot of decorating!

Since the Light of the world has come, lights strung across the roof only "shout it from the housetop." Candles and candelabra, stars and starlight, gifts and giving, songs and sonnets, light and lightheartedness, angel cookies and wise-men ornaments—all are consistent with what transpired on our little planet two thousand years ago . . . present your decorating and decorations to the Lord as a tribute to Him.

Almost every Christmas we decorate almost every thing in our house. However there have been years when the decorations were simple and few. Either way the spirit of Christmas prevailed with warmth, celebration, love, and adoration for the baby Jesus.

a medley of Ideas

Deck the halls with boughs of holly, fa la la la la la la la la.

Hang one large bell or several little bells on the inside handle of your front door.

When our daughters were young, they loved to wrap a baby doll in "swaddling clothes" and place "baby Jesus" in a basket filled with straw.

Tie wide red ribbon or raffia bows around the backs of your dining room chairs. Add a jingle bell to the bottom of each ribbon tail for extra joy!

Jingle bells, jingle bells, jingle all the way, oh what fun it is to sit in a chair like this today!

Do you have a little red wagon? Why not use it as a place to keep some of your Christmas presents? Tie a ribbon or raffia (with a bit of green tucked in) on the handle! And pile in all of your teddy bears or dolls then tie a bow around each one. I love the whimsy of red gingham!

Tie your throw pillows with ribbon as if they were gifts. A quick and easy way to "deck the halls."

A gingerbread house makes a happy centerpiece for Christmas! Make your own or make a "creative purchase" at your local bakery or grocery store. Have fun!

Whatever you do, work at it with all your heart . . .
—Colossians 3:23

33

Fa La La La La . . .

Christmas enthusiasm . . .
we set out to decorate every corner.
—Alice Taylor

Evergreens, holly, and bolts of red ribbon go a long way in "decking the halls." One branch of holly or evergreen with a ribbon tied where foliage and stem meet is very pretty. Use a clear pushpin to attach greens wherever they will bring you and others joy!

Place evergreens and holly . . .

Across the tops of mirrors and pictures · On book shelves and hutch shelves · On banisters · In bunches—or bouquets—on the gate, doors, and windows, inside and out!

A very small bunch of greens on the doghouse (no holly here!)

Oh, this is really fun! I often write a greeting, Bible verse, or message on some of my solid-colored or decorative plates. (The ink easily washes off most plates. Experiment on the back of your plate, just in case the ink won't wash off.)

A Christmas boutonniere. Tie a narrow red ribbon to a sprig of pine, make a tiny bow for ladies and a simple square knot for gentlemen. Add a little bit of baby's breath in honor of the Christ Child, "the breath of heaven." Celebrate the season and wear one every day!

Place a large, fairly flat evergreen branch beneath a large white candle. Tie a red ribbon around the candle. Pretty simple and simply pretty!

34

. . . la la la la!

Put a **favorite plate** in a plate stand. Attach a special invitation or favorite photo to the center of the plate with tape, garnish with holly or evergreen. You could even use an especially meaningful Christmas card.

Each Christmas our little creche rests in a large evergreen branch. The thought of the holy family **cradled** in that branch brings "comfort and joy" to my heart.

Hang a green wreath with nothing more that a **red bow and a Scripture** verse tacked on the bow tail. You may prefer to wind the ribbon through the wreath; this works really well with wired ribbon. Cut greetings, verses, or blessings from old Christmas cards. What to "tack" the Scripture verse with? A tie tack, an angel pin, one pierced earring (the one you didn't lose), or glue.

A flat-backed basket with a handle has countless possibilities for Christmas decorating. Here's a **front door idea!** Fill the basket with fresh greens or 2 4-inch poinsettia plants. Keep them fresh by placing wet paper towels in a large plastic bag. Then put the bag in the basket, add lots of greens (scrunch more moist paper towels down the sides if further support is needed) and cover with sphagnum moss. Tie a **ribbon or raffia** into a bow on the handle. (Be sure to have ribbon tails the length of the basket. It looks so much prettier that way.)

Dear Jesus, as I prepare my home
in celebration of Your birth, I pray to remember
the many blessings You prepared for me.
Amen

Christmas Parties & Gatherings

At Christmas play and make good cheer,
For Christmas comes but once a year.—Thomas Tusser

A Christmas gift from the heart begins with your invitation. Its very being says, "I like you, I appreciate you, I want your company at this party!" Don't you feel wonderful when you get an invitation? I do! A party can be:

A Large Gathering with Appetizers, Cookies, and Desserts

Use name tags for a party this size. Save time for singing Christmas carols. It's old-fashioned and filled with Christmas love!

A Neighborhood Progressive Dinner

Four stops for this party: hors d'oeuvres, salad, main course, and dessert.

These wonderful things are the things we remember all through our lives.

A Candlelight Dinner Party in Honor of the Light of the World

For years Tom and I have been having a special Christmas dinner with 5 other couples. Everybody makes their very best recipes, we dress up, and have a time around the table of catching up, laughing, and enjoying all the memories we share! Coordinating our schedules is no easy task. If we can't meet for Christmas, we meet for Valentine's Day or St. Patrick's Day! We simply don't want to miss the blessing of being together.

Why not begin your own Christmas dinner party group!

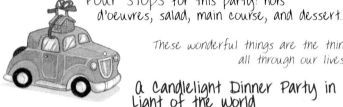

36

Out-to-Lunch Parties

Susan came up with a great idea. "Dolley, why don't we take our mothers-in-law out for a lovely Christmas lunch?" We just love our mothers-in-law and are always telling each other stories of their goodness. The lunch date is already on our calendars for next Christmas!

Just-You-and-me Parties

My mother- and father-in-law, with their joyous spirits, could make a mid-morning cup of coffee a party. An attitude of love and celebration made every coming together a party. Love for the person and celebration of the moment! Why not call your friend and invite her out for coffee and a Christmas party for two?

Parties for People who Might not Have One

The need for love, care, and celebration is with us always, but especially at Christmas. And especially for those who are isolated from Christmas activity. This is a thoughtful Christmas gift from the heart. I think of it as, well, a calling. Your church can connect you with those who would love to have your help! Be sure to include a tangible gift such as backpacks for children, food boxes for the hungry, or pen, paper, and stamps for the elderly. Follow the light of Jesus in your loving service.

Happy Birthday Baby Jesus Parties for Children

A tea party for girls and a pizza party for boys. Have a cake for the newborn King and sing, sing, sing "Happy Birthday to You!"

Work Parties—No "Bah, Humbug" Here!

Maybe you're not the party planner, but you'd still like to do something "sweet" for Christmas. How about bringing Christmas candy to work beginning December 1? My daughter Candy loves to celebrate . . . everything. A basket of wrapped (no germs this way) candy sits on her desk at work for every holiday. Let's just say she's never lonely!

> It's "the little things that count" they say,
> A little kindness every day.
> And one by one as they increase,
> Bring love's sweet gifts of joy and peace!

College Parties

Send your college student back to school after Thanksgiving with a Christmas party pack of paper plates, cups, napkins, special cookies, and candy.

> Ding Dong! Merrily on high . . .
> In heav'n the bells are ringing . . .

Christmas Tea Party Reunion

Barbara and Debbie came up with this idea when our daughters were seniors in high school. We didn't want to lose each other and so . . . the C.T.P. Reunion!

This year, we sat around Barbara's living room and enjoyed teacakes, cookies, candy, and steaming pots of peppermint and cinnamon tea. Too much fun!

Why not begin a C.T.P. Reunion? Or you could have . . .

a Christmas Luncheon

Christmas love and Christmas joy
abound around the table.
Invitations are desired . . . .
ask as many as you're able!

A dear friend has an annual Christmas luncheon with good food, a small Christmas gift, and her unabashed love! There's always a Christmas discussion question to draw us into conversation and mutual blessing! For example: what gift did the Lord give to you this year? Or, what gift have you given to Him? We run the gamut of emotions, the most prevalent being joy!

Simply done and having fun
is much better than not done at all!

Prepare the food if you have the time. If not, and your budget allows, make "creative purchases." Begin with good bread or rolls. Then buy several chicken Caesar salads (one per person is always too much), toss them together in a large salad bowl, and viola . . . . Christmas luncheon is served! A "Yule Log" ice- cream cake makes a great dessert. For an extra special touch put whipped cream in a small bowl and serve it with the coffee and sugar.

Have gentle music playing, the fire going (only if you have a fireplace!), hot apple cider, and a little something to munch. The table discussion could revolve around "the reason for the season" or my favorite, "what's your best childhood Christmas memory?"

You may wish to ask each lady to bring one wrapped gift within a certain price range for a gift exchange. This is really fun, and it's nice to leave with a little momento from the time spent together.

Strawberry Trifle

"Please Bring Your Strawberry Trifle" One of the first times I brought my Strawberry Trifle to a party, a man picked up the bowl and went around asking, "Do you want any more of this?" After getting clearance from every guest, he ate what was left! It's been a favorite for years, and now I hope you'll make it a tradition too!

Use a large glass bowl or a traditional trifle bowl with a pedestal. The layers of butter cake, strawberries, custard, and whipped cream are too pretty not to see! If time is short the day of the party, you can make the trifle a day ahead.

1 box butter-recipe golden cake mix
Bird's Custard mix (if you can't find custard mix, use vanilla pudding)
1 pint whipping cream
Stabilizer for whipped cream (see the Candy Cane Cake on page 30). You can make the trifle without it, so don't worry if you can't find it.
Powdered sugar
Vanilla
2 16-oz. boxes of frozen sliced strawberries, defrosted
A 12" length of 1/2-inch-wide red ribbon
A little snip of evergreen

Prepare the cake according to directions. Bake in a 9x13 baking pan. Cool. Mix the custard according to directions, plus 1/2 cup more milk than the directions call for. After custard is cooked, remove from heat and stir in 1 tsp. real vanilla. Cool slightly.

Pour the strawberries into a bowl other than the one you're using for the trifle. Make a very narrow slice around the edge of the cake so you won't have any hard crusts. Now cut the down the middle of the cake length. Cross cut into rectangles which are about 2 1/2-to-3" wide.

Place 1 layer of cake rectangles in the bottom of the bowl. You may have to cut some smaller pieces to make the layer even. Spoon strawberries and juice evenly over the cake. Spoon an even layer of the custard over the strawberries. now start all over again until you have filled the bowl. Be sure to leave space for the whipped cream. (Chances are you'll have some leftover cake.) Cover the bowl with foil and put in the refrigerator to cool.

Whip the cream until peaks begin to form and then begin adding powdered sugar. If you use the stabilizer follow the directions on the package. Continue whipping the cream until stiff. when completely cool cover the trifle with whipped cream. Then mound and swirl more whipped cream on top!

Garnish your trifle with a little Christmas tree—take a sprig of evergreen and cut the green from the bottom of the stem to create a tiny "tree trunk." Tie a bow around the tree trunk. Just before serving, place the "tree" flat in the middle of the trifle and curl the ribbon around it.

You're Invited to The Party
We're excited as can be
We'll sing some Christmas carols
and decorate the tree!
What shall we have with coffee?
Oh my, oh my, let's see. . . .
Oh yes, your Christmas Trifle
will do quite perfectly!

The Flowers of Christmas

Glad tidings we bring to you and your kin;
Glad tidings for Christmas and a Happy New Year.

Fresh flowers speak volumes of love, thoughtfulness, and care. How do you feel when someone presents you with flowers, either a single stem or a whole bouquet? I'm guessing your answer will be, "pretty special." That's certainly true for me.

I associate certain flowers with very dear memories. Such as the time Candy had a single red rose delivered to Tom and me for a wedding anniversary. Her sweet gesture was the perfect gift!

Poinsettia

Originally grown in Mexico where it is called "Flower of the Holy Night." The "hall decking" just doesn't seem complete without at least one poinsettia, the Christmas flower. This beautiful Christmas plant comes in a variety of colors. Buy one for the coffee table or two for either side of the front door, but . . .

a true gift from the heart comes when you buy one for a friend and give anonymously. Just drop it by her front door, ring the bell, and run!

Drop, ring, and run! Too much fun!

Roses

Roses are a popular flower choice for the holidays, and I'm sure there is a rose in your favorite hue. But whatever the color, a rose always communicates love! When our loved ones live far away sending a bouquet of Christmas roses says it all—wish you were here or I was there. I love you. Blessed, blessed Christmas.

Seek roses in December . . .—Lord Byron

At Christmastime I put a single red rose with pine and baby's breath in each of my daughter's bedrooms. The red rose is for the baby Jesus so sweet. His sacrifice saved us. The evergreen pine for the everlasting life He gives us. And baby's breath for the "breath of heaven" that came to us with open arms of love from the manger to the cross.

Some years I've given my girls a single white rose instead, for the new year and new Beginning, capitalized because it's so awesome to have a new Beginning!

If you, then, . . . know how to give good gifts to your children, how much more will your Father in heaven give good gifts to those who ask him!—Matthew 7:11

If you live in a warmer climate, please don't overlook the flowers and greens available in your garden. Ivy, white bougainvillea, pyracantha, and evergreen branches are but a few of the plants that can easily be used for Christmas arrangements and also tied on last-minute gifts.

43

narcissus or

This graceful, willowy white flower has a sweet, pungent fragrance. The first year I had paper whites in our home the girls didn't like the fragrance; now they miss it if I don't plant the bulbs on time! And planting on time is key if you want to give narcissus flowers as holiday gifts.

Time Table for narcissus Bulbs

Plant On		For Blooms On
October	15	Thanksgiving
October	21	Hanukkah
November	14	Christmas
November	20	New Year's Eve

Paper whites for Gifts

You can plant the bulb in just about anything. Let your imagination be your guide. You can plant one bulb or a bunch in a:

- cozy teacup
- garden-variety clay pot
- oversized coffee cup with saucer
- ceramic or silver teapot ✴
- brass container ✴
- special vase designed specifically for growing bulbs

✴double-line with plastic or bubble wrap

Paper Whites

How to Plant and Grow

The bulbs can be planted in pebbles, gravel, potting soil, sand, any supportive material. Plant the bulb(s) so that the base is anchored but the top of the bulb is peeking out. I surround my bulbs with moss for a finishing touch. Keep it wet, not soaking, just wet. Place in the dark until there's about 3 inches of growth, then bring it out. They do best in bright, indirect light when blooming.

As your narcissus begins to grow to its full height it may begin to lean over. Just tie a couple of lengths of raffia into a bow around the middle of the plant. Or if you have planted it in something elegant use gold cord or narrow ribbon.

And please know that many nurseries and flower shops carry paper whites already grown. If you haven't the time to plant you can always make a "creative purchase"!

Flowers are lovely; love is flower-like;
Friendship is a flowering tree.—Coleridge

Dear Friend,
Thank you for planting prayer in the garden of our friendship.
HAPPY NEW YEAR!

If you missed giving Christmas gifts, don't feel at all guilty. We're grace filled here! A narcissus (under these circumstances, buy one) planted in a pretty container would make a happy, Happy New Year gift!

We're only here for a short visit. Don't hurry. Don't worry.
And be sure to smell the flowers along the way.
—Walter C. Hagen

45

"Almost" Flowers

Think about using ordinary, around-the-house things to deck the halls. Here are a couple of ideas, but let your imagination be your guide. Have fun hunting for hidden treasures in your own home!

Cranberries

Cranberries? Yes, they make a great anchor for fresh flowers. Use a clear vase and fill it about 2/3 of the way with the berries, then water and flowers. For an extra special touch, tie a length of ribbon for pretty, raffia for country, or gold cord for elegance around the vase.

Pearls

Buy a string of trim-the-tree pearls at a craft or Christmas store, and use them in floral arrangements the same way you would the fresh cranberries. This type of arrangement looks especially elegant with a gold cord or French ribbon tied around the vase.

Tom brings me flowers and I make him creamed corn. Creamed corn? Yes, creamed corn! He just loves this recipe, and I hope you do too!

"Thank you for the Flowers, Honey" Creamed Corn

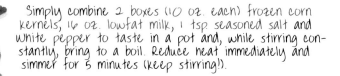

Simply combine 2 boxes (10 oz. each) frozen corn kernels, 16 oz. lowfat milk, 1 tsp. seasoned salt and white pepper to taste in a pot and, while stirring constantly, bring to a boil. Reduce heat immediately and simmer for 5 minutes (keep stirring!).

In another pot, melt 2 tbs. butter and blend in 2 tbs. flour, add to the corn, mix well but gently, and remove from heat. Put the creamed corn in your favorite covered (so it stays hot until the last kernel) serving dish. Enjoy!

memory making & Tradition Keeping

*Traditions are ribbons of memories and love
holding family and friends together.*

The Four Family "Traditional" Christmas Potluck

The Carlson, Gundlach, Storm, and Wilson families have been celebrating a traditional Christmas potluck together for the last 10 years! Here's a little blueprint of how the evening goes. I hope it will be helpful to you in creating your own traditional Christmas party!

The first ingredient in this recipe for fun and good cheer is simplicity. make a phone call invitation.

menu
Appetizer · Green salad · Hearty soup ·· Good bread
and ice-cream sundaes with Auntie Teri's Hot Fudge Sauce
You don't even need to ask. Here's the recipe;
you're going to love it!

Love is coming back and going forth! your house or mine?

Auntie Teri's Hot Fudge Sauce

Combine 1 tbs. butter, 1 1/2 squares unsweetened chocolate, 1 1/2 cups granulated sugar, and 3/4 cup half and half in a saucepan. Bring to a boil, reduce heat, and let it boil gently for 3-4 minutes, stirring occasionally. Remove from heat and let stand for 5 minutes before serving. This is a third generation treat—loved by all ages!

whatever you do, don't wash that pan until someone has had a chance to get the last of the chocolate out with the "traditional" finger-licking "tradition"!

The evening begins with free-flowing visiting and picture taking! There are a lot of no ways! and exclamations from all the kids during this time. After dinner, we sing carols, and one by one, answer questions pulled from a basket that help us know each other even better. We truly are family as we sing praises to the newborn King.

Some of the questions were: What would you say about the person on either side of you? • What is your funniest Christmas memory? • What's an intangible gift you could give to someone?

The last song was "O Holy Night" and although I know this song well, it was as if I was hearing it for the very first time.

...O HOLY NIGHT...

Long lay the world in sin and error pining,
Till he appeared and the **soul felt its worth.**

I believe every soul in that home felt its worth in the tradition of Christmas love and adoration for the newborn King! What a blessed, love-filled evening!

Take Your Family to a Christmas Cultural Event
The Bible tells us that things wear out and get lost. You can't lose an experience. It stays in the heart! And if you have boys, I promise they'll never forget the Christmas you took them to the nutcracker ballet!

A Christmas Parade
Why not gather your family and go to your town's parade this year! The price is right, and you'll be making a memory too!

make an Event of a Christmas Outing
Our parents would take my sister, brother, and me
into Boston every Christmas for a traditional day
of shopping, eating, and enjoying all the decorations
throughout the city. One of our favorites was the
life-sized nativity scene on the Boston Common. It
seemed so real!

A dear Christmas memory was made when we
stopped to visit friends. While the grown-ups talked,
Mrs Ward served us gingersnaps and milk. She
seemed genuinely interested in all we had
done that day. I never eat a gingersnap that I don't remember her sweet
smile and gentle manner.

The Nativity Scene, Creche, Crib, or Stable
Every Christmas my mother carefully arranged the nativity scene and with great
tenderness put the holy family in place. This is one of
my dearest Christmas memories! And the tradition contin-
ued when Tom and I bought our first creche.

When Candy was 3, our best gift would come
from her. One night I noticed something different
about the baby Jesus. . . . He was wrapped in a
Kleenex! "Mommy, He looked like He was really
cold" and so she wrapped Him in the tissue. "The
little Lord Jesus laid down His sweet head" once
again, only this time He was a little warmer.

Bless all the dear children in Thy tender care . . . .

New Pajamas for Christmas
Here's a unique slant! When Karen was growing up,
all 12 cousins got the very same style of pajamas
on Christmas Eve. And a "traditional" snapshot was taken
of smallest to tallest!

Grandpa's Box Sled

On Christmas Eve, Grandpa always managed to find a large, sturdy box and make a "traditional" indoor box sled. What a delight to see him pulling the "one-Grandpa open sleigh" around the house with a gleeful baby gurgling, "mo, Gampa, mo!"

Holiday Clothing

You look for it every year. That Christmas tie your uncle has been wearing for as long as you can remember. Holiday apparel is a gift of good cheer to all you come in contact with. So get out those jingle bells and tie them on your shoes or purse or . . . and remember what "Annie" sang, "You're never fully dressed without a smile!"

Don we now our gay apparel . . .
Fa la la la la, la la, la, la.

Christmas Music

Music carries us to memories of Christmas past, calms us in Christmas present, and centers us in joy and reverence for celebration of the Savior's birth. Gather tapes and cds, and put them in a basket for easy access. Two of our favorites are a speedy version of "Jingle Bells" and The Messiah by Handel.

Hallelujah! Hallelujah!

. . . . A Christmas music video brings a concert right to our home and is a joyful gift for shut-ins.
. . . The sacred sound of family and friends: children giggling, carols "plunked" on the piano, kitchen whirs and splashes and "what can I do to help?" And the sweet song of "The food is ready, everybody come now."

make Peace—make merry and Bright

Peace on the earth, good will to men,
From heaven's all gracious King.

By sharing our time and resources with those who need help. A dear friend told me of a young widow with three small children who had no resources for Christmas presents. "Helpers" bought a tree, decorations, and presents. The helpers saw the mother as a selfless angel, and that's the spirit they honored. On Christmas morning her oldest child shouted with glee, "mom, there's a present with your name on it!" The little package was her only gift, a small silver angel suspended from a dainty necklace!

God loves a cheerful giver.—2 Corinthians 9:7

And traditions are gifts, gifts from the heart to the heart. Here are some of my favorites!

A Christmas Cookie Party for Kids from "One to Ninety-two"

make batches of "The Perfect Sugar Cookie" and freeze them until partytime. Gingerbread boys and girls are good make-ahead cookies too! Partytime! Set out pots of frosting—red, blue, white, green, and yellow—toothpicks (good for tiny dot accents) and inexpensive paint brushes.

You can buy tubes of frosting and set those out as well. Add decorations of tiny red-hot candy hearts, sprinkles—multicolored, green, red, yellow—and whatever other cookie decorations you like. Provide pretty Christmas paper plates, cellophane, and ribbon for your guests to package their gift cookies in.

Perfect Sugar Cookie Recipe

3/4 cup butter (or 1/2 butter, 1/2 regular margarine,
   equaling 3/4 cup) softened

2/3 cup granulated sugar   1 tbs. light cream
1/4 tsp. salt   1 1/2 tsp. vanilla extract
2 egg yolks   2 cups unsifted, all-purpose flour

Measure butter, granulated sugar, and salt into a bowl. With electric mixer at medium speed, beat until mixture is smooth. Add egg yolks, cream, and vanilla. Beat until fluffy, about 2 minutes. Gradually add flour, stirring with wooden spoon until well combined and smooth. With hands or spoon, shape dough into a ball. Place on waxed paper. Flatten dough and wrap. Refrigerate 2 hours or overnight. Dough will be firm.

Preheat oven to 325 degrees.

Divide dough into fourths. On lightly floured pastry cloth, with floured rolling pin roll out to 1/4-inch thickness. Press together any cracks at edge. Cut with assorted cookie cutters. Place cookies, 1 inch apart, on ungreased cookie sheets. If you want to add sprinkles to top of cookies, lightly brush top of uncooked cookies with egg white, then sprinkle on decoration.

Bake 12-15 minutes, or just until edges of cookies are light golden. Remove to wire rack or bread board. Cool completely.

Traditions continue as traditions
because the memory is sweet.
You want to hold on to it forever and ever,
and that's how it becomes,
as Tevya of Fiddler on the Roof says,
"Tradition!"

The Christmas Tradition of your Ethnic Heritage

It's important to keep in touch with our ethnicity, because it's part of who we are as family. Ask your "grand" generation about their Christmas memories, and you're sure to discover an ethnic tradition. Here's ours—feel free to share it with us!

my husband's family is Swedish, and on Christmas Eve, we have a smorgasbord. In Sweden "Santa Lucia" is traditionally celebrated December 13 with a daughter wearing an evergreen wreath of lights (pretend—for safety) on her head as she serves sweet rolls and coffee to her family. Grandma and Grandpa were pleasantly surprised when Candy and Katie upheld this tradition.

Children's children are a crown to the aged . . . —Proverbs 17:6

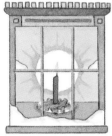

The Irish tradition of a candle in the window on Christmas Eve continues in our home today. my grandmother, Nora Catherine Foley, immigrated to America and brought this precious tradition with her. The candle indicates room in your home and heart for the baby Jesus. In Ireland long ago, the candleholder was a turnip! today we use an electric candle for safety.

Originated in England, crackers are party favors made out of paper, filled with little token gifts, and a colorful tissue hat! we've worn these festive hats at many a Christmas dinner, "cracking up" at how silly we are!

when we lived on opposite sides of the country, my aunt jane often wrote to me, "may we sit at the same table soon." I now understand the depth and love of those words as never before . . . may we break bread, talk, laugh, be with our loved ones, and say merry Christmas one more time!

It's a Wrap! & Tabletops!

To get the full value of a joy, you must have somebody to divide it with.—Mark Twain

Why table settings and gift wrapping together? Because it's so much fun to tuck our gifts in places other than under the tree.

Gift wrapping is one of my favorite things to do. It's a wonderful time to pop a video of *It's a Wonderful Life* in the VCR and enjoy! Or have a **wrapping party** for two and invite a friend! You'll have each other's company and help too—"Could you please hold this while I tie a bow?"

I'm a recovering perfectionist and gift wrapping is a lot more fun than it used to be. Truth be known, everything is a lot more fun this side of the impossible—perfection! As my daughters say, "Mom, and the point is . . . ?" The point is to use a free hand with your wrapping and you'll have a lot more fun! Think fun! Think joy! Think merry!

Pick and Choose What You Like Best
Okay, here's what you'll want for our "It's a Wrap" endeavor . . .

. . . white, red, and green tissue paper. New tissue makes your gifts look crisp and well presented.

. . . a roll of clear cellophane can be used really well for food items, see-through "want to give them to you right now" gifts, and gift baskets. Everything looks special in cello and the crinkly noise is fun too!

. . . Gift bags with handles. I prefer shiny white or grocery-store-brown for a country look. Or try clear cellophane bags.

54

. . . Wrapping paper. My favorites are solid colors—shiny green, white, and red. You can write the To . . . and From . . . right on the package with a glue pen. Sprinkle with glitter. For elegance try white paper, gold or silver glitter, and white ribbon. Use your imagination and have fun!

. . . Comics from your newspaper—Sunday and during the week too! Color for little kids, black and white for big . . . red ribbon for this one!

. . . "Brown paper packages tied up with string, these are a few of my favorite things." Use twine and make a tag out of last year's Christmas cards, and you'll be giving the perfectly wrapped gift to your friend who is conservation minded!

. . . Gold glitter—go crazy! . . . Silver glitter—go crazy again!

. . . Gift tags can be used for place cards at your holiday table. Put actual gifts on the table or tie ribbon around napkins with a gift tag attached, and you have a place card and napkin ring too.

. . . Gift stickers. I like to put gift stickers right in the middle of a cello-wrapped bread that is tied on both ends.

. . . Trim last year's Christmas cards for gift tags or decoration.

. . . A bag of excelsior or craft straw. Use the same way you are using the tinsel or in gift baskets. Create a base filler with newspaper and then cover and fill with straw.

. . . Lollipops, candy canes. Great tie-ons for your gifts.

. . . Jingle bells. Put one or two inside the gift and your present will jingle and . . . jangle!

. . . Bolts and bolts of ribbon—and whatever else may catch your fancy!

. . . A package of small gold cord—reserve this for elegance! Or combine with red, green, or white ribbon for a festive presentation.

. . . Gold and/or silver tinsel. Just two or three pieces tucked in a Christmas bow—instant twinkle!

Table Setting Is a Gift . . .
"Simply Beautiful or Beautifully Simple"

At Christmas time there are so many choices for tabletop surprises! Best of all, we'll use things we already have. Come on, let's set the table!

Christmas is coming, the geese are getting fat,
Please to put a penny in the old man's hat,
If you haven't got a penny, a ha'penny will do,
If you haven't got a ha'penny, God bless you!

First Things First

. . . Tablecloth. Solid colors give a bold background for tableware. However, don't rule out patterns (especially checks and candy-cane stripes).

. . . Place mats. I purchased 4 sets of Christmas place mats and napkins, 2 of each pattern, about 10 years ago. They still look really pretty.

. . . Quilt. I use one every Christmas. Its primary colors just shout joy. I set the "quilt" table with large red plates that I bought at an off-price "as low as the price is ever gonna get, lady" store.

. . . . One of my favorite settings has runners "running" all over the table. Seriously! Put 2 runners down the length of your table and cross over with two more runners in the middle for a total of 8 places at your table. Use moiré or another dressy fabric and they will look just like woven ribbons!

God bless the master of this house,
likewise the mistress too;
and all the little children
that round the table go.

Dishes and Glassware

Use regular-sized dinner plates as chargers for luncheon-sized paper plates. You'll still get a pretty table, but the cleanup will be much easier!

Don't be afraid to mix and match different patterns. It's a perfect look for a big table. The big table . . . I want to tell you about the big table!

This year Tom and I decided to surprise the family with one big table. We did it for Grandma, knowing she would love it! We emptied the living room of most furniture, rented 4 tables and white tablecloths, then pushed the tables together. We set the table, alternating china patterns, silverware, and crystal too.

I can't remember a meal when people remained seated so long! No missed jokes, conversations, or stories. It was a lot of work. Whew, what a job! But it was worth every minute of planning, moving, and "setting" to create a unique memory, especially for Grandma who said, "This is the best party the family has ever had!"

For a buffet table, place silverware in a napkin, tie with a ribbon, and nest in a basket or across a large plate. But don't stop there. Tuck a little bit of green or a candy cane beneath the ribbon—just to say "we're glad you're here!"

If your water glasses have stems, tie a ribbon around them. This is a great way to serve a dessert—so festive! Teri and I bought the same green stemmed goblets long ago, knowing that we could combine our collections for large parties.

A friend in need is a friend indeed.

Gifts as Table Favors and Place Cards

Simply place in the middle of a plate or above it . . . a Christmas tree ball, personalized with glue and glitter . . . Little loaves of bread wrapped in cello and tied with a pretty bow make great "little gifts". . . Candles, small candy boxes, a bell, a tiny box with a Christmas pin inside, or a small book of inspiration or poetry.

Candles

Candlelight symbolizes Jesus, the light of the world. Have candlelight lead the way to the dining room. The glow can come from candles in the middle of the table, or one at each place—a "remember our time together" gift.

Centerpieces

Fill a pretty bowl with small gifts for your guests. Or with ornaments, fruit, nuts, or pinecones. Put 2 evergreen branches with stems underneath the bowl. Candles on either side too, and you're set!

Gingerbread Boys and Girls

Create a centerpiece with greens, little poinsettias or narcissus, and gingerbread kids. Write each guest's name in white frosting, and add frosted characteristics of the guests, such as glasses, blond hair, mustache . . .

A Bowl Piled High with Red Apples

How pretty! Add one apple at each place. Core the apple and put a 6-inch-tall white candle in it—fun! Light the candles, turn off the lights, and invite your guests to a candlelit, "you're the apple of His eye" Christmas meal.

He shielded him and cared for him;
he guarded him as the apple of his eye.
—Deuteronomy 32:10

58

Sheer Elegance

Use white and gold as a backdrop for your dishes and china. Wrap small gifts in shiny white paper, tie with a gold ribbon, and add a gift tag to serve as a place card. Put a gift in the center of each plate. Then put 3 poinsettias or narcissus (4-inch containers) in individual brass planters, in a straight row, in the middle of the table. Place white and gold candles on either side of the flowers. Unite all of it with wide wired ribbon, curling in and out. Use narrower ribbon for napkin rings.

Teddy Bears

Put a gift in the hands of a teddy bear (or 3 bears) and it's Christmas! Sprinkle candy canes and other sweet treats all around, and place a runner or evergreens beneath everything! Don't forget the candles and ribbon!

When Kim began to nibble the candy, his wife, Anne, whispered, "Honey, you're eating the centerpiece . . ." That's what it's there for, but who knew?

Be sure to tell your guests that the centerpiece is edible!

A nativity scene or creche is the sweetest centerpiece of all, not only for our Christmas tables but for our hearts as well! Make a precious place card for this meal by tracing a heart on the paper of your choice with a heart cookie cutter and personalizing each one.

For God so loved Karen
John 3:16

Don't let the "ghost of Christmas perfection" rob you of happy times with your friends and family. These ideas are here to help and inspire you toward coming together with those you love, lots and lots!

The gathering heart not only loves, it blesses too!

Happy Birthday,

Joy to the world! The Lord is come; Let earth receive her King; Let every heart prepare Him room.

Christmas carols sing out, "glory to he newborn King," "This is Christ the King," "On Holy Night . . . it is the night of our dear Savior's birth." And yet it's so easy to forget that this is a Happy Birthday, Baby Jesus time of celebration in the midst of all the shopping, cooking, baking and party making!

Anne Graham Lotz once gave a Christmas message that stirred my heart. She spoke of giving a birthday gift to Jesus of being still, praying, and asking Him what gift He would like from you. Anne said that when she takes the time to ask, He answers.

What if my friends gave me a party and I wasn't invited? Suppose I saw one of the guests who said, "Dolley, glad to see you! We had a birthday celebration for you. We exchanged presents and spoke of how much we all love you. And we do. Have to go now, bye!"

We've talked a lot about giving gifts to others. However, there is a precious gift you can give yourself that will change your life and influence all your gifts from the heart forever. It's the gift of Jesus. Yes, Jesus, the Son of God, wants to reign within your heart and life. Ask Him, "Come into my heart, Lord Jesus; Come in today . . . Come into my heart, Lord Jesus."

Baby Jesus!

And Jesus has gifts He brings . . .

The Gift of Forgiveness
We've all made mistakes and poor choices. There isn't one person on earth who hasn't. Jesus offers us forgiveness, a new beginning, and eternal life!

The Gift of Love
Do you know there's nothing you can do to get God to love you any more or any less? He just loves you!

The Gift of Affirmation
God has a unique and beautiful blueprint for each and every life. "For I know the plans I have for you," declares the Lord, "Plans to prosper you and not to harm you, plans to give you hope and a future." (Jeremiah 29:11).

If you don't know the Lord Jesus, I pray you will take this very moment to ask Him into your heart. If you do know Him, why not pause to recommit your heart to Him?

Jesus fills our hearts with new blessings and gently places us in the family of God. It's why Jesus came to earth and died for our sins. O the wonder of that first Christmas night . . .

O holy night; the stars are brightly shining
It is the night of the dear Savior's birth.

It was Christmas Eve 1955 in New England.
I was a child and awoke in the middle of the night.
The quiet was like sacred music. I ran to the window, hoping to catch a glimpse of Santa and his reindeer. What I saw was much better.

While we were sleeping, heaven covered our neighborhood in a soft, thick blanket of snow! The moon shone in perfect beams and the sky looked like velvet. Thoughts of Santa vanished and turned to how much God must love us to have sent snow for Christmas! I clearly felt the love of God as I stood there at the window.

O holy night how you blessed the heart of a little girl so long ago, and the blessing remains in the memory of this woman's grateful heart.

You can't orchestrate this kind of experience for your child or loved one, but you can pray for it. Ask Jesus to bless your loved ones with a lifelong memory of His care for everything in their precious lives. And that this special memory would be an anchor for their relationship with Him.

HOPE

Jesus, the Gift from God's Heart to ours.
In Jesus, the possibilities are endless and will last from here to eternity. Gifts from the heart are like that, they keep on giving and giving.

Every good and perfect gift is from above,
coming down from the Father.
—James 1:17

Happy new year!

Thou crownest the year with thy goodness . . .
—Psalm 65:11 KJV

The new year's issue of a magazine captured my heart. The cover was a picture of newly fallen snow with one little pine sprig popping up in the middle. It looked like hope! Renewal! And another chance to do life right . . . God bless second chances!

Forget the former things; do not dwell on the past. See, I am a new thing! Now it springs up; do you not perceive it? I am making a way . . .
—Isaiah 43:18-19

For me, the snow symbolized a "white as snow" forgiven heart, and the little pine sprig an evergreen reminder of being "ever" renewed by God's love. Sitting on the threshold of a new year is the perfect opportunity to drop grudges, forgive, ask to be forgiven, and begin anew!

Gifts of forgiveness

. . . Send a new year greeting card to break the ice and warm the hearts of both the forgiver and the "forgivee."

. . . Forgiveness is the most expensive gift of all, but merciful forgiveness is priceless! Do you realize how much energy it takes to hold on to unforgiveness? A lot! Maybe you're righteously indignant! Make a tight fist with your right hand. Takes some doing, . . . righteous indignation! Holding on robs us of blessings and of being a blessing!

Release, bless and be blessed in giving your "white as snow" gift of forgiveness.

We're over it.—Katie Carlson

Our hearts, our hopes, our prayers, our tears,
Our faith triumphant o'er our fears,
Are all with thee—are all with thee!
—Henry Wadsworth Longfellow

Gifts of Encouragement

Send a new year's note and affirm special talents or skills. You could also write, "I know the Lord has wonderful plans for you; this is your year." Encourage them even more by including a verse such as "May the God of hope fill you with all joy and peace as you trust in him, so that you may overflow with hope by the power of the Holy Spirit" (Romans 15:13 NIV).

Therefore encourage one another and build each other up.
—1 Thessalonians 5:11

Another gift of encouragement is to begin a support or prayer group. Meet once a week or every other week and be specific about your goals and objectives, not only for the group but for your new year as well. Commit your loving trust to each other and your meetings to prayer, counsel, and God's Word.

And let us consider how we may spur one another
on toward love and good deeds. Let us not give up meeting together,
. . . but let us encourage one another.—Hebrews 10:24-25

God's richest blessings to you and yours
From me and mine this new year and always.

Dalee